Floriculture
Leader and Youth Education, Grades 3–4

Floriculture

Leader and Youth Education, Grades 3–4

Kathryn S. Orvis

Purdue University Press
West Lafayette, Indiana

Copyright © 2025 by Kathryn S. Orvis. All rights reserved.
Cataloging-in-Publication Data on file at the Library Congress.

978-1-62671-331-4 (paperback)
978-1-62671-332-1 (epdf)

Cover image: Courtesy Purdue University Ag Communications.

Any figures available in color appear that way in the e-book format.

A previous version of this book was published by 4-H.

Contents

Preface and Acknowledgments..................................vii

1. Let's Plan...1
    1A. Somewhere Over the Rainbow...Garden................1
    1B. A Cut Above the Rest..4

2. Dig In...7
    2A. Digging In...the Soil..7
    2B. Transplants for a Speedy Start................................10

3. While You Wait...11
    3A. Blooming Seeds..11
    3B. Flower Power..16

4. Watch Out...19
    4A. Healthy Plant Parts..19
    4B. What's Buggin' You?..22

5. Now What?...25
    5A. Blooming Rainbow..25
    5B. Blooms A-Round..31

6. Imagine That...34
    6A. An Introduction to Floriculture..............................34
    6B. Plants Around the World......................................36

Glossary..39

References 42

Record Sheet 43

About the Author...45

Preface and Acknowledgments

Getting Started

Congratulations, a young person has asked you to be his or her helper. Your role as a helper is very important to the total educational experience of the young person. Not only will you be providing encouragement and recognition, you will also be the key person with whom the young person shares each of the experiences outlined in this activity guide.

The *Floriculture* educational series is full of exciting hands-on activities that focus on growing and using flowers and plants. Youth will also have fun creating flower garden plans, growing flowers, and designing basic arrangements. The curriculum is designed around five major categories: planning, growing and caring for plants, exploring science, floral design, and career exploration. These concepts are organized into six chapters: "Let's Plan," "Dig In," "While You Wait," "Watch Out," "Now What?," and "Imagine That."

A total of four pieces are available in the *Floriculture* curriculum series. The four activity guides have been designed to be developmentally appropriate for grades 3–4, 5–6, 7–9, 10–12, respectively, but may be used by youth in any grade, based on their project skills and expertise.

The Experiential Learning Model
The experiential model and its five steps are used in each activity in this guide as a means to help youth gain the most from the experience.

The five steps encourage the youth to try to do the activity before being told or shown how (experience). As the helper, you'll want to help the youth describe what they experience and their reaction (share). You can use the questions listed at the end of the activity to help the youth:

- Discuss what was most important about what they did (process).
- Relate the life skill practiced to their own everyday experiences (generalize).
- Share how they will use the life skill and project skill in other parts of their lives (apply).

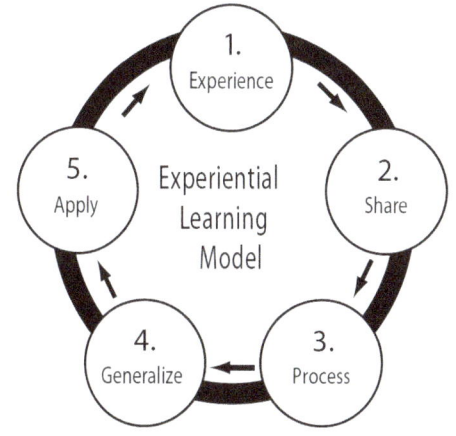

Pfeiffer, J.W., & Jones, J.E., "Reference Guide to Handbooks and Annuals"
© 1983 John Wiley & Sons, Inc.
Reprinted with permission of John Wiley & Sons, Inc.

Acknowledgments
Many thanks to all who helped create the *Floriculture* series.
Writing: Kathryn S. Orvis
Design team: Jeff Jones, Roberta Crabtree, Richard Beckort, Janet Berndt, Duane Martin, Dave Garrett, Mary Lou Hayden, and Mary Welch-Keesey
Student assistants: Stephen L. Meyers, and Ashley L. Mueller
Clerical support: Terry Saunders, Jane Robertson, and Andrea Mrozinski
Editor: Rebecca Goetz
Graphical Layout: Jeannie Byers, Cassi Halsema, and Jessica Seiler
Additional content providers and reviewers: B. Rosie Lerner, Mary Lou Hayden, Mary Welch-Keesey
Photos: Joan Crow, Stephen L. Meyers, Kathryn S. Orvis, Erin Shanley, and Mary Welch-Keesey

1 Let's Plan

Somewhere Over the Rainbow...Garden

ACTIVITY 1A

Materials Needed:
- Pencil
- Ruler
- Seed and garden catalogs

Time Needed:
- 30 minutes

Flowers add color to your home. Look around your yard and find a spot that needs color. It's waiting for a flower garden. You can put a flower bed near your house or by the back fence, around a small tree or like an island in your yard. Check the spot where you plan to put your flower bed to see how much sun it gets. Is it on the side of a building? North, south, east or west? Under a tree? The amount of sunlight will determine which plants will grow best in the site you choose. Is there a water faucet or hose near by?

- **Life Skill:**
  Planning and organizing, making decisions, valuing diversity

- **Project Skill:**
  Plan a rainbow garden

Try This

Plan a garden. It can be any shape. You might try a Rainbow Garden with all the colors of the rainbow in it. You can shape it in a half circle to look like a rainbow. Put your tallest plants at the back of your garden and plant one row of each color. You may want to plant flowers that bloom for a long time so it will look nice all summer. These flowers are called annuals. To learn more about **annuals,** look at the article on the next page of this activity.

Look through seed catalogs for pictures of flowers you would like to grow. Many seed catalogs provide beautiful pictures so you can see what the flowers will look like. Catalogs, as well as the backs of seed packets, give information on growing the seeds. They also tell you how tall each plant will be.

A few plants you might like in your Rainbow Garden are:

Color	Plant
Red	zinnia, snapdragon
Orange	marigolds, calendula
Yellow	marigolds, sunflower
Green	envy zinnia, coleus
Blue	forget-me-nots, bachelor buttons
Indigo/Violet	salvia, larkspur, pansy

Draw your flower garden plan here or on a separate piece of paper. Be creative and label where you will put each plant.

MY RAINBOW GARDEN PLAN

Location of my garden will be: _____

Size of my garden is: _____

Flowers I will plant are: _____

The height and color of each flower I chose is:

Flower	Height	Color

Number of seed packets I need to buy: _____

I will get the seed from: _____

Annuals

Annuals provide color all summer long. An annual is a plant that only lives one summer. It blooms and blooms to make many seeds for next year. Annual plants grow to be many different sizes. Sunflowers can grow to be 6 feet tall—that's taller than you! Pansies will be only 6 inches tall, just a little taller than your ankle.

Some annuals grow and flower best in the sun, but others prefer shade.

Some annuals grow easily from seeds planted directly in the ground. Other annuals are easier to grow from plants you purchase at a store. These small plants started indoors, often in a greenhouse, are called "transplants."

Blossoming Discoveries

Tell your project helper how you decided where to put your garden. Did someone help you?

_____
_____
_____
_____

Explain why it is important to plan ahead.

_____
_____
_____
_____

List two other times you used planning and organizing in your life.

_____
_____
_____
_____

Describe a time when you needed help from a parent or adult before you could plan.

_____
_____
_____
_____

Dig Deeper

See what you can discover from a seed packet. The front of a seed packet usually has a picture of the plant the seeds will become. The back side of the packet will give you important information on planting your seeds. Some of the things you will see on the back side of a seed packet include:

Planting Depth
Some seeds need sun to sprout. Others do not. Always read the packet **planting depth** and plant your seeds as deep as it tells you.

Days to Sprout/Days to Germination
The number of days it takes for your planted seed to sprout (or germinate) may be very different for each kind of flower. Some flowers may take more than 14 days to sprout. Some may sprout only a couple of days after you plant them. Your seed packet will tell you how many days it should take your seeds to germinate.

What the Seedlings Look Like
Some seed packets show small pictures of what your seedlings should look like after they sprout. This helps you find them. That means you can recognize which plants are weeds and should be pulled while they are young, and which are your plants and should be left alone.

Time to Plant
Do your seeds like cool or warm weather? The seed packet tells you when you should plant your seeds so that they can live and grow well. If you plant seeds too early, they may die from cold weather or a frost. If you plant them too late, they may not have enough time to grow and flower before the first frost of the fall.

Location
Does your plant need shade or sun to grow best? Plants like all different amounts of sunlight. If the seed packet does not tell you the best place to plant your seeds or plants, ask your project helper to help you find this information.

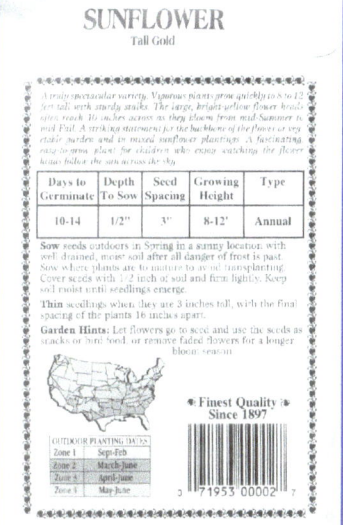

Let's Plan / 3

A Cut Above the Rest

ACTIVITY 1B

A cutting garden not only gives you outside color, it also allows you to bring that color inside to enjoy. Flowers in a cutting garden are chosen for their ability to keep on blooming and because their flowers stay nice after being cut. Some plants are easy to grow from seed. Others aren't, and you should buy those plants, **transplants**, already started from a greenhouse. Most seed packets have codes to tell you if flowers do well when cut. So do garden seed and plant company websites.

- *Life Skill:*
  Planning and organizing, making decisions

- *Project Skill:*
  Plan a cutting garden

Materials Needed:
- Pencil
- Ruler
- Seed and garden catalogs

Time Needed:
- 30 minutes

Try This

Draw your cutting flower garden plan here or on a separate piece of paper or on your computer. Be creative and label where you will put your plants. Remember what you learned in activity 1A, "Somewhere Over the Rainbow...Garden," about planting tall plants in back, short plants in front.

MY CUTTING GARDEN PLAN

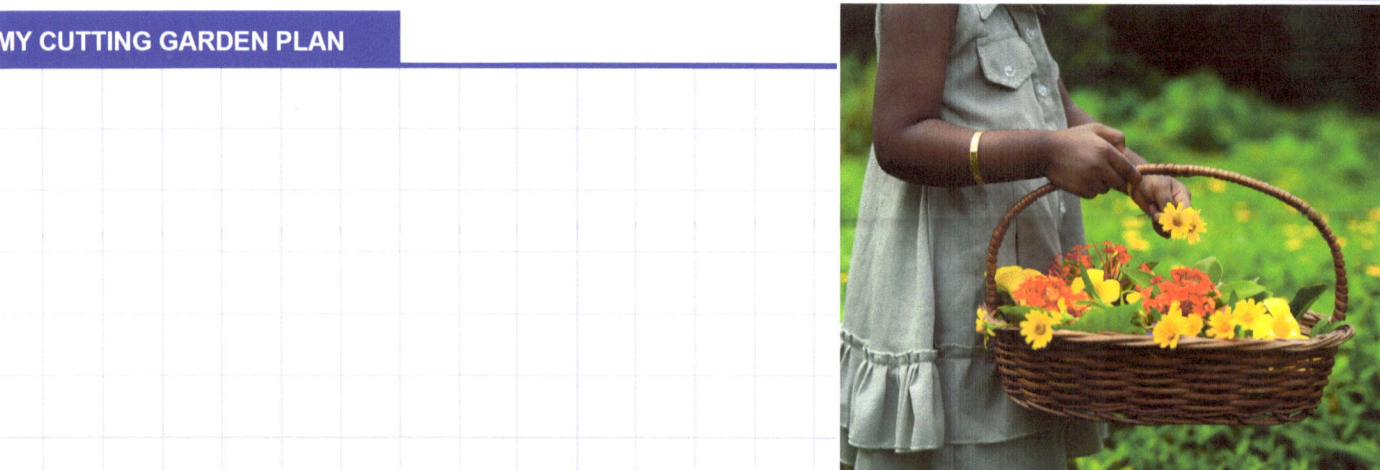

4 / Floriculture Leader and Youth Education, Grades 3–4

Transplants

Transplants grow indoors or in a greenhouse before they are planted in your yard. Flowers are grown as transplants for many reasons. Some are grown as transplants because their seeds are too small to plant outdoors. Others may be started as transplants because they require a longer time to flower.

When selecting transplants, choose plants that look healthy and show no signs of stress such as yellowing leaves. Each transplant should have lots of roots and a sturdy stem. Look for plants that are compact and not spindly (tall and weak). You will learn more about how to transplant your flowers in Chapter 2.

Use this table or create one of your own to plan your garden.

My Cutting Garden

Location of my cutting garden will be: _____

The size of my garden will be: _____

The flowers I will plant	From seed	From transplants	The cost

I will get my seeds or plants from: _____

Examples of flowers to grow from seed	Examples of flowers to grow from transplants
zinnia	statice
marigold	celosia
sunflower	snapdragon
cosmos	petunia
larkspur	geranium
calendula	
bachelor's buttons	

Let's Plan / 5

Dig Deeper

Pinching

Often a plant is bushier and has more flowers if you just pinch it. **Pinching** is removing the tips of the plant. The tip of a plant is the part that grows the most. When you pinch it, the plant will grow out more and up less. To pinch a plant, squeeze your fingers together taking the top inch (or less) of the plant's tip between your thumb and forefinger. The tip of the plant should break off easily. Be careful, and don't harm the parts of the plant below the tip when you do this.

It is best to purchase plants that aren't yet blooming and pinch them back so they will branch out and have more flowers. One experiment to try is to buy several plants of the same kind. Pinch some back and leave others as they are. Which one has the most flowers after one week? Two weeks? One month?

Blossoming Discoveries

Tell your helper how you will use transplants in your garden. Would transplants be cheaper than planting seeds in your garden?

_____
_____
_____
_____

Give at least one reason why people need to plan ahead for expenses.

_____
_____
_____
_____

Name three expenses your parents need to plan for.

_____
_____
_____

List two things in your future where you'll have to make a plan that includes considering expenses.

_____
_____

2 Dig In

Digging in...the Soil

ACTIVITY 2A

Materials Needed:
- Tape measure or yardstick
- String
- Shovel
- Rake
- Organic matter (manure or compost)
- Hoe
- Several short stakes
- Seeds

Time Needed:
- 1 hour

Growing flowers is easy and fun! Flowers can be grown just about anywhere, even in containers on the porch. Most require sun, but some grow in partial or even full shade.

Before planting, make sure your soil is ready or good for planting. Is your soil hard to dig in? Flowers will not grow well in hard soil. The soil needs to be soft and loose to allow water to drain and roots to feed and breathe. If your soil is hard, you can add organic matter to improve the soil.

Organic matter is made from things that have been alive or that come from a living plant or animal. Examples of organic matter are decayed leaves and manure.

Are you ready to dig in? Before you start, make sure you have a plan. You can use the rainbow garden you designed in Activity 1 or create a new plan. Your garden can be any shape, such as a rectangle or circle. Use a garden hose to lay out the curves of your garden. Stakes and string help you make straight lines.

- Life Skill:
  Completing a project or task, motivating yourself, communicating
- Project Skill:
  Planting a garden

Try This

In this activity you will plant and grow a flower garden. Please check with your project helper to decide where to place your flower garden.

1. Lay out your flower garden plot using a tape measure or yardstick.
2. Mark the area with the stakes.
3. Tie string from stake to stake, or outline the shape of your flower garden plot with a garden hose.
4. Start at the outside edge of your plot, dig down about 12 inches with a shovel, and turn over a shovelful of earth.
5. Continue digging across the width.
6. Try not to step on the soil that has been turned over, because it will pack down.
7. Break up large chunks. Pull out grass, weeds, and large rocks.
8. Add organic matter. Add about 2 inches and work it into the soil.
9. Smooth the soil with a rake.
10. Decide the proper plant spacing.
11. Plant seeds according to packet directions.
12. Water gently until soil is wet.

Seed Planting Information

Seed Spacing
How far apart should I plant my seeds? The back of the seed packet should tell you. Remember from the "Let's Plan" chapter that even small seeds can grow to be very big. If seeds are planted too close together, they may not all get enough light, water, or nutrients. A general rule for **planting depth** is to measure the seed's length, then plant it twice as deep as that. If the seed packet does not tell you how far apart or deep to plant your seeds, ask your project helper to help you look in books or catalogs, or on the internet to find this information.

Watering
Seeds need water to sprout, grow, and live. After you plant your seeds, water them until the ground around them is thoroughly wet. Keep the soil around your seeds moist until they sprout. If it rains, you may not have to water them that day. If it is really hot outside, water your flowers early in the morning. After your seeds sprout, you can water them less.

Rain is measured in inches of water that fall. Most plants and flowers like to have one inch of rain each week. Ask your project helper to help you learn how much rain has fallen each week. If it rains only a little or not at all, you will have to water your flowers.

Weeding
Weeds are plants that are growing where you do not want them. Weeds do not look nice and may be harmful to your flowers. Weeds take water, sunlight, and nutrients away from your flowers. This is why you should remove weeds from your flower garden. You can do many things to have fewer weeds in your garden.

Some gardeners put organic matter on top of the soil as well as in the soil. This organic matter, called **mulch**, shades the soil, helping it stay moist. Mulch also shades out weeds. You can add mulch, such as compost or bark, on top of the soil to keep weeds from growing in your flowers. When putting mulch in your flower garden, remember not to cover your flowers. The mulch should be about 3 inches deep to keep most weeds away.

Another way to get rid of weeds is to use a garden tool called a hoe. Hoes gently uproot the weeds. When using a hoe, don't go too deep or you might harm your flowers' roots.

Organic Matter and Compost

What is organic matter? Organic matter is nutrition for the soil. Organic matter keeps earthworms and other life working in your soil. It also holds moisture for your plants to use.

What is compost? Compost is organic matter that is so finely broken down that you can't tell if it was originally grass, leaves, or bark. Some gardeners make their own compost so they have organic matter to add to the soil.

Blossoming Discoveries

Tell your project helper what important information you learned about planting a flower garden.

_____
_____
_____

Explain why it is important to know the steps in planting a flower garden.

_____
_____
_____

List what you learned about the importance of following the steps or instructions in order when completing a task.

_____
_____
_____

Describe how, in the future, this activity could help you teach others in your community about how to plant a garden.

_____
_____
_____

Dig Deeper

1. With your helper, go to a local garden center and talk to an employee to learn about other types of organic matter.

2. Plant seeds in different types of soil and compare the differences in plants. Also, try different depths.

3. While waiting for seeds to sprout, design markers to identify your flowers. Rocks, wooden stakes, or other recycled materials are good options.

Transplants for a Speedy Start

ACTIVITY 2B

Once your garden is prepared, you can add plants by purchasing small plants, called **transplants**, from the local garden center or greenhouse. You will find familiar plants that you may have started from seed in your own garden, and some that are more unusual.

Special care is needed when transplanting your new plants. Their small **roots** can lose water quickly, and their tender leaves are easily sunburned. The best time to transplant is late in the afternoon or evening, when the sun is not as bright, and on a cool, cloudy, windless day so the new plants don't dry out. Be gentle in handling the plants. They are young and tender and can be easily broken. Do not remove a plant from the container until you are ready to put it into the ground. The roots can dry out very quickly.

- **Life Skill:**
  Completing a project or task, being responsible

- **Project Skill:**
  Transplanting plants into a garden

Materials Needed:
- Tape measure or yardstick
- Rake
- Garden markers
- Shovel and trowel
- Transplants and seeds of the same plant

Time Needed:
- 30 minutes

Preventing Transplant Shock

Try This

Transplant your new small plants to your garden or container.
1. Dig holes wide and deep enough for each root ball, loosening the soil around the edges of the holes.
2. Gently remove each plant from its container, making sure not to pull on the plant to remove it. If it is in a peat pot or pellet, you can plant the entire container. Make sure that you move each plant with as much soil as possible. Try not to damage the roots.
3. Set the plant upright in the hole and fill all the space around the roots with loose soil. Do not pack soil too tightly. Place your new transplant at the same depth or slightly deeper than it was growing before.
4. Water gently until moist.

Watch your transplants carefully. Don't let the hot sun or windy days make the shock of transplanting worse. If it is very sunny, make newspaper tents over the plants for protection. If it is windy, cover the plants with cardboard boxes or thin cloth. If frost is predicted, cover plants with newspaper tents or boxes or cloth. Uncover just after the sun comes up the next morning.

10 / Floriculture Leader and Youth Education, Grades 3–4

Blossoming Discoveries

Tell your project helper how you used transplants in your flower garden.

_____
_____
_____
_____

Explain why it is important to handle transplants properly.

_____
_____
_____
_____

Name other activities in your life that require you to complete tasks.

_____
_____
_____
_____

Describe how caring for your transplants can help you learn to care for other living things.

_____
_____
_____
_____

Dig Deeper

1. Comparison: Plant seeds directly into the ground. At the same time, plant transplants of the same kind. Compare the sizes of the plants and number and sizes of blooms at one-week intervals. Is there a difference?

2. Transplants are often used in decorative pot plantings. Find a pot or other interesting container and plan what you would want to plant. Then plant it and observe.

While You Wait

Blooming Seeds

You can grow many different flowers from seeds. You can buy seeds from a garden center or a seed catalog. Your friends and neighbors may give you seeds from plants they have grown.

What's in a seed that helps it grow into a new plant? What do seeds need to sprout and grow? In this activity you'll look inside a seed. Then, you'll place seeds in different situations to see what they need to grow.

When conditions are right, a seed will sprout. We call this process **germination**. Germination has several different steps. These steps always take place in this order:

1. The seed takes in water through its **seed coat**.
2. The seed swells and gets larger.
3. The **root** appears.
4. The **shoot** and **leaves** appear.

For a seed to move through these steps and germinate, it must have water, air, and warmth. You can do tests (**experiments**) to find out what happens if the seed gets too much (or too little) water or no air, to learn how a seed responds to different temperatures.

- Life Skill:
  Understanding systems, using the scientific method, keeping records
- Project Skill:
  Understanding seed germination

ACTIVITY 3A

Materials Needed:
Part 1:
- 2–3 Lima or kidney beans
- 1 cup water
- Glass
- Pencil
- Paper

Time Needed:
- Preparation: 24 hours
- Day 1: 30 minutes
- Day 2–10: 15 minutes per day

Try This
Part 1: Inside a seed

Look at a kidney or lima bean seed. Guess what you think is inside the seed.

1. Soak the bean in water overnight (24 hours).
2. Ask an adult helper or friend to help you carefully peel the outer coat from one of the seeds. Then, split the seed in half with your fingernail. Draw what you see.
3. Refer to the glossary, then label these parts of your drawing: seed coat, **cotyledon**, and **embryo**.

12 / Floriculture Leader and Youth Education, Grades 3–4

Materials Needed
Part 2:
- Several paper towels
- Jar with lid
- Long sheet of paper (or several taped together)
- Pencil
- 40 lima or kidney beans (soaked in water overnight)
- Several sealable plastic bags
- Water
- Magnifying glass (optional)

Part 2: Discovering—What do seeds need to grow?

Experiment 1

1. *Ask a question and make a guess (a **hypothesis**).*
   What happens if seeds don't get enough water during germination? Predict what you think will happen:

   _____

2. *Test your guess.*
   Dampen two paper towels. Fold each once, then place 10 soaked seeds on each towel. Fold both towels again, over the seeds. Place one paper towel in a plastic bag. Do not put the other towel in a plastic bag. Keep both towels together in a warm place for a week. Record (write down) the date you start both experiments.

   _____

3. *Get the answers.*
   Make two folding "books" so it's easy to write down what you see. Fold a long strip of paper so it looks like an accordion. Use one book for the seeds in the plastic bag and one for the seeds that aren't in a plastic bag.

   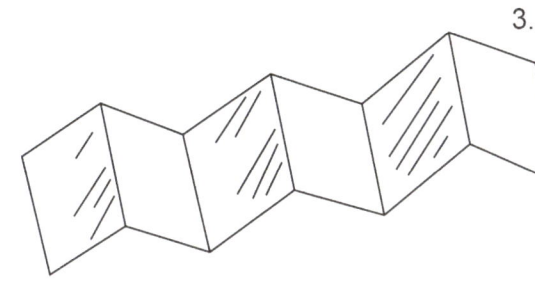

   Look at the seeds every day. Each day, use one section of the folding book to draw a picture of the seeds. Show all changes. Record the date and how wet or dry the paper towels are.

4. *Compare your answers with your guess.*
   After a week or 10 days, unfold the two "books" and compare them. Did the seeds do what you guessed they would do?

   _____

5. *Decide what it means (draw a **conclusion**).*
   What does this tell you about seed germination?

   _____

   _____

Experiment 2

1. *Ask a question and make a hypothesis.*
   What happens if seeds don't get enough air during germination? Predict what you think will happen:

   _____

2. *Test your hypothesis.*
   Dampen a paper towel. Fold once, then place 10 soaked seeds on the towel. Fold the towel again, over the seeds, then place it in a plastic bag. Put the other 10 seeds in a jar filled with water. Put the lid on the jar. Keep both the towel and the jar together in a warm place for a week. Write down the date you start this experiment.

   _____

3. *Get the answers.*
   Make two folding "books" so it's easy to write down what you see. Fold a long strip of paper so it looks like an accordion. Use one book for the seeds in the plastic bag and one for the seeds in the jar of water.

   Look at the seeds every day. You should be able to see the seeds in the jar without taking them out of the water. Each day, draw a picture of the seeds on one section of your folding book. Carefully draw any changes. Record the date of each entry in your book.

4. *Compare your answers with your hypothesis.*
   After a week or 10 days, unfold the two "books" and compare them. Did the seeds do what you guessed they would do?

   _____

5. *Draw a conclusion about your experiment.*
   What does this tell you about seed germination?

   _____

   _____

   _____

Scientific Method

We use an experiment like the ones in this chapter to find an answer to a question (e.g., What happens if a seed does not get enough water?). First, we guess the answer to the question. The guess is our hypothesis. Next, we do our experiment to see if our guess was correct. This is called the Scientific Method. It is OK if your guess is different from your results. Scientists often make exciting discoveries when their results don't match their guess.

There are eight steps in the Scientific Method.

1. Ask a question.
2. Get information about the question.
3. Make a guess (hypothesis) about the answer to your question.
4. Test your guess. The test is an experiment.
5. Get the answers (the results of the experiment).
6. Compare your answers with your guess.
7. Decide what your answers mean (conclusion).
8. Tell others what you found.

When you drive to the store with an adult, you are following a certain path on the road to get there. The Scientific Method works the same way. You must follow a certain set of steps to get from the question to the answer.

Blossoming Discoveries

Tell your helper your hypothesis, your results, and your conclusions from the two experiments.

_____
_____
_____
_____

Explain why is it important to know what conditions help seeds germinate.

_____
_____
_____
_____

Where else, besides school, can you use your skills of observing?
List three.

_____
_____
_____

How will you use this skill in the future?

_____
_____
_____
_____

Dig Deeper

1. With your helper, go on a scavenger hunt in your kitchen to find examples of seeds. Compare the seeds you find by size, color, and texture. Go to the grocery store and see if you can find other seeds. What is the largest seed you found? The smallest? Do you eat seeds like those you found?

   Go on a scavenger hunt for seeds in your garden or yard. The seeds may be inside fruits or flowers. Look for fruit and flowers in the garden, then break them open to see if they have seeds.

2. Most plants grow best if they are not close to lots of other plants. How do seeds get from their parent plant to a place of their own? Some seeds like dandelions have plant parts that catch the wind. This means they can be blown far away from the flower. Other seeds have special parts that grab onto the fur of animals and travel to new homes. Lots of seeds are inside fruits. When fruits are eaten by animals, the seeds are carried around inside that animal. The animal later "plants" those seeds away from the parent plant. Find several seeds and/or fruits and see if you can guess how each gets to a new home.

3. With your helper, design an experiment to show how temperature influences seed germination. Make sure you follow the scientific method. From your results, when would you plant a seed outdoors?

Match each word in the list below with its definition.

Word	Definition
Seed coat	a tiny plant complete with leaf, stem, and root parts
Cotyledon	to begin to grow; sprout
Embryo	contains temporary food the plant uses until it can grow up to make food with its leaves
Germinate	contains the stem and leaves
Shoot	protects the embryo

While You Wait / 15

Flower Power

What Is a Flower?

Do you enjoy looking at plants with lots of flowers? Everyone does! Flowers help our gardens look beautiful. They help the plants, as well.

Flowers are the reproductive parts of plants. That is, they are responsible for making seeds. Seeds **germinate** and grow into new plants. Most flowers contain four different parts that help them successfully make seeds:

Sepals—Sepals are the outer covering of the flower. If you see a flower while it is a bud, before it opens, the parts you see are the sepals. They help protect all the other parts of the flower. Most sepals are green.

Petals—Petals are often the showy part of the flower (however, the sepals can sometimes be showy). They may be brightly colored and are often large.

Stamens—These are the male parts of the flower. A stamen has a long stalk and an anther on the end that produces **pollen**. The **anthers** often look a little fuzzy and may be colored brown, black, or yellow.

Pistil—This is the female part of the flower. The top part is called the **stigma**. It is sticky so any pollen that lands there will stick. Below the stigma is a long, thin part called the **style** that leads to a swollen area called the **ovary**. Seeds are formed inside the ovary. As the seeds ripen, the ovary swells and becomes the **fruit**.

Each plant has a different type of flower. Different flowers have different numbers of sepals, petals, stamens, and pistils. Sometimes the sepals or petals are all joined together; sometimes they are separate. Petals of different flowers can be different colors, sizes, and shapes. Because each type of plant has unique flowers, we can tell what type of plant we have by its flowers.

- *Life Skill:*
  Communicating, reasoning, processing information, solving problems

- *Project Skill:*
  Understanding flowers and pollinators

ACTIVITY 3B

Materials Needed:
Part 1:
- A flower
- Pencil or colored pencil
- Paper
- Eraser

Part 2:
- Several flowers
- Pencil
- Paper
- Friend or group of friends, parent, or 4-H group
- Eraser

Time Needed:
- 45 minutes

Simple Flower

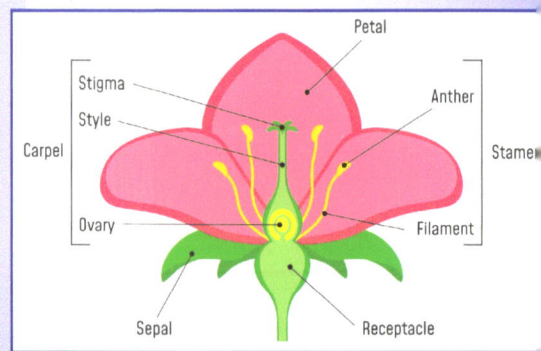

Pollination

For seeds to form, the male part of the flower must get to the female part of the flower. That is, the pollen from the stamen must get to the stigma. This transfer of pollen to the stigma is called pollination. From the stigma, pollen travels through the style to the ovary where seeds are made.

How does the pollen move? One way is wind. In spring, many plants bloom and there is lots of pollen in the air. If you have spring hay fever, you probably are reacting to the pollen from plants that are pollinated by the wind.

Animals also move pollen from flower to flower. These animals are called pollinators. Some animals like certain types of flowers. For example, butterflies and bees like flowers that cluster together to form a flat surface. Flowers of daisies, butterfly bush, and sedum are very popular with these animals. Some flowers produce a scent to attract their pollinators. Other flowers produce nectar, a sugary liquid, that many animal pollinators eat. In exchange for food, the flowers are pollinated.

Pollination is important for people who grow ornamental plants and food crops. Apple orchards must have a plentiful supply of pollinators or the flowers will not be pollinated efficiently. If the flowers are not pollinated, no fruit will form. Can you imagine an apple orchard without apples?

Try This

Part 1:

With your helper, find a flower and carefully take it apart to find the sepals, petals, stamens and pistil. Then, draw the different flower parts. Carefully count the number of parts and label your drawing.

Part 2:

Play a game with a friend. Get four or five different flowers. Look closely at each flower and write down a description that includes what size it is, how many petals and sepals, and the color of the anthers. Don't use color to describe the petals. You may also describe how it feels to touch, how it smells, how large each part is, and other physical characteristics.

Show your friend(s) all of the flowers, and then read each flower description. See if he/she/they can correctly guess which flower you are describing.

While You Wait / 17

Dig Deeper

The scent of a flower will often attract an animal pollinator (such as an insect) to that flower. Visit a large garden and smell a number of flowers. Visit the garden during the day and, if you can, again in the evening. How many of the flowers have a strong scent? A few, many, or all? What type of animals are attracted to them? Why might some flowers have scent only in the evening rather than during the day?

The scent of flowers is attractive to humans, too. Do you like certain scents? Flower scents are used in perfume, bath lotion, and other personal care products. Ask your helper to let you smell lotions, etc. Which do you like? Which don't you like?

If you have a flower garden (or if you can visit one), walk slowly through the garden and observe which animals come to which plants. Visit at different times of the day. Are the animals different? Is more than one animal attracted to the same flower? How is the flower attracting those animals? Do some research in a library or on the Web to find which animals like which types of flowers.

Some gardeners grow plants to attract specific animals. Pick an animal that is attracted to gardens and find out what it likes and dislikes. Then, use a seed or plant catalog to pick the plants you would grow in your garden to attract that animal.

> **Are insects and butterflies animals? Yes! Other pollinators include bats and birds.**

Blossoming Discoveries

Tell your project helper some of the words you used to describe flowers and their parts.

_____
_____
_____
_____

Explain why is it important to understand how pollen moves.

_____
_____
_____
_____

Describe what you learned about communicating when you played the game where you described flowers.

_____
_____
_____
_____

In the future, how can you use what you learned about communicating to explain complicated concepts to other people?

_____
_____
_____

Watch Out

Healthy Plant Parts

ACTIVITY 4A

Materials Needed:
- A garden to visit
- A garden center (or another place where lots of plants are) to visit
- A gardener you can interview
- Pencil
- Paper

Time Needed:
- 1 hour

Plant Parts

What are the parts of a plant and what does each part do?

Each plant has different parts—roots, stems, leaves—that must work well for the plant to grow strong and healthy and produce flowers, seeds, and fruit.

What are roots?

A **root** is much more than something that holds a plant in the ground. Roots give a plant the water it needs. How? Water in the soil enters the root and is carried up through the root to the stem and then to the plant's leaves and flowers.

A **root** is so important since it is the first thing a sprouting seed grows. (Think back to Activity 3A.) Roots don't take up just water—they take up minerals as well. These minerals are nutrients for the plant, like the vitamins and minerals your body needs to stay healthy.

When roots are working well, they are usually white and have no odor. Sick roots will be brown and mushy and may smell rotten.

What do stems do?

The water and minerals taken up by the roots travel up the **stem** to the **leaves** and flowers. Food produced by the plant's leaves travels back down the stem to other parts of the plant and to the roots. The stem is like a super highway for water, minerals, and food.

Stems hold up the leaves so the leaves can best use sunlight to make the food the plant needs. Stems also make new leaves and **flowers**.

Stems also help a plant stand up straight. In your body, your spine and other bones help keep you straight. In plants, water does this job. That's why when a plant needs a drink of water, it will droop and fall over. When you give it water, it stands straight again.

Healthy stems stand straight and strong and have no sunken or funny colored areas. Stems that have sections missing are not healthy.

What are the plant's leaves for?

Leaves use sunlight to make food for the rest of the plant. Healthy leaves are usually green. Leaves that are yellow, white, brown, or spotted may not be healthy. Leaves with pieces taken out of them are not healthy.

What are flowers for?

Flowers help the plant make new plants. The flower forms the fruit and seeds inside the fruit. Flowers are healthy when they mature to become fruit. Flowers that aren't healthy may have bad color or spots. They may fall off before the fruit is formed.

- Life Skill:
  Communicating, interacting socially, visualizing information
- Project Skill:
  Understanding plant parts and what sick and healthy plants look like

Try This

Part 1:
Visit a garden and look for an unhealthy plant. What tells you that there is a problem? Describe the symptoms a unhealthy plant might have.

Part 2:
Visit a garden center or other place where lots of plants grow. Talk to someone who takes care of the plants about how they keep the plants healthy. Ask them what they do, as well as what they don't do. Ask them to point out plants that are not healthy. Ask them what they think is causing the problem and what they will do to fix it. Are any of their problems like the ones you found in Part 1?

Part 3:
Visit a garden center or other place where lots of plants grow. Look for plants that naturally have **variegated** (for more information on variegation, see the section on the right) or unusually shaped or colored leaves. Think of clues that might help you tell if the plant is unhealthy or just naturally variegated or colored.

Sick or Healthy

To tell if a plant is unhealthy, you must know what it looks like when it's healthy. This is easy if it's a familiar plant, but what if you've never seen it before? Reference books and pictures will help you learn what a plant should look like. Look in the library or on the internet for some examples.

Some plants aren't sick, but look different. Here are some unusual things you might find:
- A plant grown in sun may look different than the same plant grown in shade. A plant grown in shade may have larger leaves and longer stems when compared to the same plant grown in the sun.
- Instead of being completely green, some leaves are a combination of two or more colors, such as yellow and green or white and green. We call such leaves variegated. A green and yellow variegated plant may look sick, but it's really not.
- Some leaves have unusual shapes. There are many different types of Japanese maple trees, each with leaves of a different shape, perhaps even a different color. Diseases and insects can cause leaves to be the wrong shape, but sometimes these different shapes are normal. You may decide to grow a specific plant just because you like the leaf shape or color.
- Some plants (tulips, daffodils, and potatoes) have swollen stems. If you dig up the plants, you'll find these swollen stems, in addition to the roots. It might look like these stems are sick roots, but they aren't.

Blossoming Discoveries

Describe to your project helper how you decided if a plant was healthy or not.

_____

_____

_____

_____

Explain why it is important to understand how your plants communicate with you.

_____

_____

_____

_____

Describe what you learned about communication.

_____

_____

_____

_____

In the future, how can you use what you learned about communicating to find a better way to solve a problem?

_____

_____

_____

_____

Dig Deeper

We eat many plant parts: fruits, leaves, flowers, stems, roots, and the seeds. Below is a list of vegetables. Write the name of the plant part you eat. (Hint: There is one vegetable for each plant part.) With your helper, take a trip to the grocery store and see if you can find other vegetables that are roots, stems, seeds, fruit, flowers, or leaves.

Vegetable	Plant part I eat	Other vegetables I found that are this plant part
Carrot		
Asparagus		
Peas		
Lettuce		
Tomato		
Broccoli		

What's Buggin' You?

ACTIVITY 4B

As soon as you step outdoors, you'll find insects. Insects are everywhere—on flowers, in trees, creeping among the blades of grass, and sometimes in our houses. Some people think all insects are creepy and bad. Certainly no one likes to be stung by a yellow jacket or to find ants in their pants! While some insects deserve the label "bad," many insects help gardeners, and many more are neutral, neither good nor bad.

Insects may help gardeners by transferring pollen from plant to plant. Without these pollinators, seeds and fruit would not form. Other helpful insects attack and kill insects that harm our flowers and vegetables.

Bad insects, called insect **pests**, damage plants. Some do this by chewing pieces out of plants. If this type of insect attacks your garden, you may see holes in leaves or bites taken out of fruit. These insects have mouths designed for chewing. Other insect pests suck liquid from plants, stealing food and water, which plants need to be healthy. Leaves attacked by these insects may have tiny yellow or white spots on them. They may be puckered or oddly shaped. These insects have mouths that are specially designed to pierce plants and suck out liquid.

It's important to make sure an insect is really hurting your plants before you try to get it out of the garden. Observe carefully how the insect is interacting with the plant. Talk with your project helper or other adult, or consult a reference book to learn about the insects you see and their impact on your garden.

☐ Life Skill:
Making decisions, valuing diversity, solving problems

☐ Project Skill:
Identifying insects in your garden (beginner)

Materials Needed:
- An area with lots of plants—such as a garden, field, yard, woodland, etc.
- Insect net (optional)
- A jar with holes in the lid for collecting insects
- Paper
- Pencil
- Magnifying glass (optional)

Time Needed:
- 1 hour

In the world, there are more insects than any other type of animal. If you piled up all the insects on earth, they would weigh more than all the people. All of these insects share certain characteristics that tell us they are insects. These are:
- Hard body with an exo skeleton
- 3 body parts (head, abdomen, thorax)
- 6 legs
- 2 antennae
- Compound eyes in the adult
- Wings (Not all insects have wings but many have 4, some only 2.)

Try This

You can find information on identifying insects on the internet or other books or 4-H resources.

1. With your helper, collect several insects and look at them closely. Draw a picture of at least three, and label the parts. Use another sheet of paper, if necessary.

2. Watch some insects in a garden. What are they doing? Are they helping, harming, or neutral? Make a list of what you see and any clues you used to decide what type of insect each is.

Type of insect	Clues used to identify	Good, bad, neutral	Effect on plant

3. Look for an insect pest in your garden. Find some damaged plants. Then, write a description of the damage, tell why you think an insect caused the damage, and decide if the insect had chewing or sucking mouth parts. Share your discoveries with your project helper and look up any answers you don't know.

_____

_____

_____

_____

Dig Deeper

1. Working with your helper, make your own insect net. You will need an old pillowcase, a wire coat hanger or length of heavy wire, and an old broom handle or piece of wooden dowel rod (or something similar to make the handle), and duct tape. First untwist the coat hanger into one long piece of wire. On the bottom seam of the pillowcase (the open end) cut a small hole. Insert the wire through the hole and slide it through the seam of the pillow case, leaving about 4 inches of the wire sticking out on both ends. Use those ends of wire to attach to your handle (old broom handle or dowel rod). You can lay the wire along the handle and use duct tape to attach it. Now you can practice collecting insects in your very own net! List four kinds of insects you caught and where you found them.

2. How do you control insect pests in the garden? Find a gardener you respect and ask him what he does. Write down four different ways he controls insects and share these with your project helper.

3. All insects go through multiple stages of life—egg, larva, adult, pupa. What is the life cycle of an insect? How is the life cycle of a ladybug different from the life cycle of a butterfly or a grasshopper? Investigate these questions with your project helper.

Blossoming Discoveries

Tell your project helper what insects you found and what they were doing with or to the plants in the garden. Explain how you decided whether each insect was helping or harming your garden. How did you decide if it was neutral?

_____
_____
_____
_____

Describe why it is important to learn about the different insects in your garden.

_____
_____
_____
_____

Explain what you learned about collecting information before making decisions.

_____
_____
_____
_____

Have you ever made a decision without having all the facts? In the future, how will you go about collecting information when you have a decision to make? How will you decide that you have enough information to make a decision?

_____

5 Now What?

A Blooming Rainbow

ACTIVITY 5A

Materials Needed:
- Flowers and greenery
- Vase (clean)
- Scissors
- Bucket of water
- Floral conditioner

Time Needed:
- 1 hour

Creating an **arrangement** of flowers you grew yourself requires a little extra effort and care. Flowers you select from your garden should be healthy, have a sturdy straight stem, have perfect petals, and have clean leaves with no damage or disease. You should put them directly into warm water when you cut them, so take a bucket with you to the garden. It is also best to harvest flowers from the garden in the early morning or late evening to prevent stress to the flowers and limit the amount of water lost by the plants.

Once you have collected flowers from your garden to use in an arrangement, you will need to take some extra steps before you use them. This process is called **conditioning.** Conditioning is preparing the cut plant materials from your garden to last a long time in the arrangement. It helps the flowers by allowing the stems to fill up with water and get a good drink, which can help them last twice as long.

Flowers you can easily grow in your garden that are good for simple arrangements include sunflowers, marigolds, snapdragons, and zinnias. You can also look around for some interesting plant materials to use as greenery. Ferns, hosta leaves, iris leaves, and twigs are just a few examples. Greenery for **bud vases** can have many different colors and textures.

You can also buy flowers to make an arrangement. Flowers bought from a florist will already be conditioned.

- Life Skill:
  Practicing creativity, completing a task, valuing diversity, visualizing information
- Project Skill:
  Simple arrangement or container based on "rainbow garden"

1. Insert greenery.

2. Place focal flower.

3. Place second flower.

3. Place filler flowers.

Simple Bud Vase

Try This

Conditioning Flowers from Your Garden

To condition flowers, cut the flower's stem on an angle while holding underwater. This works easiest by filling a bucket full of warm water and holding the stem down underwater while cutting it with a sharp knife or pair of scissor or pruners. Cutting underwater prevents air bubbles from clogging the stem and makes it easier for the flower to drink. Allow the flowers to rest in another bucket of warm water that has **floral preservatives** added (see "Dig Deeper") for at least an hour before using them. This gives the flower time to drink up as much water as it can hold. Once the flower is conditioned, it is ready to be used in an arrangement. Conditioning will help cut flowers stay nice longer.

Simple Bud Vase

Before you start to arrange your flowers, you should decide how you will assemble the arrangement. Working with your helper, read the instructions before you start. Also, see information on "color" on page 28. You should also gather all the supplies you will need in one place. Fill the vase with water and add floral preservative.

As you put flowers and greenery in your arrangements, be sure to make a fresh cut on each stem just before you place it in the vase. Leave the flowers in the original container until you are ready to use them. It is best not to leave the plant materials lying on the table while you are working on the arrangement because they can dry out.

1. Insert the greenery into the vase. This is the background of your arrangement. Use just enough to help hold the flower up, but not so much that the vase is full of stems. Before inserting the greenery, remove any leaves near the bottom of the stem that would be in the water.
2. Next, place the **focal flower(s)** in the center of the greenery, in the proper proportion. Remove any leaves from the bottom of the stem that would be in the water.
3. Lastly, place one to three stems of **filler flowers** in the vase, making sure to fill any holes around the focal flowers and to balance out the arrangement.

To create your bud vase, you will need a focal flower, a filler flower, and some green plant materials. For your first bud vase, use just one kind of focal flower. For example, use only pink carnations, or only red roses, but not one red rose and one pink carnation. You will need one to three stems of focal flowers. Filler flowers are less dramatic and are usually small flowers, such as baby's breath, heather, or statice. Filler flowers help balance the arrangement and make it look full. Just one type of filler flower and one type of greenery should be used in a bud vase.

The focal flower, such as a rose, should be the focus of the arrangement. The focal flower is what provides color and interest to the arrangement. The total height of the flowers should be between 1 ½ and 2 times the height of your vase. In other words, if the vase is 9 inches tall, the total finished arrangement should be 18 to 27 inches tall. If your focal flowers are large and heavy, they may be positioned lower in the arrangement so the design will be stable and not fall over.

Blossoming Discoveries

Share with your project helper how you made your arrangement.

_____
_____
_____
_____

Describe why is it important to understand how to care for flowers after cutting them from the garden.

_____
_____
_____
_____

Explain what you learned about how to combine flowers and greenery into a pretty flower arrangement.

_____
_____
_____
_____

Think of three ways you can use this skill in the future.

_____
_____
_____
_____

Dig Deeper

Did you know that flowers are living? They still need water, light, and food to remain attractive and pretty in your arrangement. What can you do to keep your flowers healthy for a long time? Florists use floral preservative in the water to help keep cut flower arrangements looking nice for several days. Professional floral preservative has both food and something to prevent the growth of fungi and bacteria in the water. You can make a simple floral preservative at home with common ingredients in your kitchen. Here are a few recipes to try (see Purdue CES publication HO-158 for more information).

Try this experiment: get four stems of flowers, such as carnations, and put one into each of the three preservatives below, and one in just water. Observe the flowers each day. What do you see? After how many days does the flower in plain water start to die? How many days for each of the three preservatives?

	Number of days flower lasted
Mix 1 • 2 cups lemon-lime carbonated beverage • 2 cups water	
Mix 2 • 2 tablespoons fresh lemon juice • 1 tablespoon sugar • 1/8 teaspoon household chlorine bleach (a few drops) Mix three ingredients with 1 quart water	
Mix 3 • 2 tablespoons white vinegar • 2 tablespoons sugar • 1 1/2 teaspoons of medicinal mouthwash Mix three ingredients with 1 quart water	
Plain water	

Color

How do you choose which flowers to use in an arrangement? Many people choose flowers based on color. But which colors look good together?

You can use a **color wheel** to help you select colors. The color wheel is a simple way to look at colors and divide them into groups. Most color wheels have six colors—three **primary colors** and three **secondary colors**. The primary colors are red, yellow, and blue. The secondary colors are orange, green, and purple. These secondary colors are made by combining the primary colors in different ways. Red and yellow combine to make orange; yellow and blue make green; blue and red make purple. Color wheels can be found on page 33.

Some color combinations are more pleasing than others. Here are three simple ways to combine colors. We use big words to name them, but the idea behind them is simple. Think about these combinations when you choose colors for your flower arrangement or for your garden. Remember, when you choose colors for your arrangement consider all parts of the arrangement—not just the focal flowers, but the vase and filler flowers, also.

1. Use only one color. This is called a **monochromatic** arrangement. For example, you could select one red flower, then combine it with other flowers that are slightly lighter in color, like pink, or slightly darker, like burgundy.

2. Use colors that are directly opposite each other on the color wheel. These colors are called **complementary**. Complementary colors, like red and green or blue and orange, help make each other more bright or intense. They can add excitement to a flower arrangement or a garden.

3. Use colors that are next to each other on the color wheel. These colors are called **analogous**. Many people like analogous colors, like yellow and orange or blue and purple, because the colors seem to go together easily.

It takes some practice to learn how to use the color wheel. Here are some things you can do to help you remember which colors go together.

List all the ways to make complementary combinations and all the ways to make analogous combinations.

Three complementary combinations are:

Yellow and _____

Red and _____

Blue and _____

Six analogous combinations are:

Yellow and _____

Yellow and _____

Red and _____

Red and _____

Blue and _____

Blue and _____

Color is important because it affects the other parts of a design, such as the focal point. The colors of the flowers, **foliage**, and container should harmonize or seem to belong together. Flowers come in all colors of the rainbow, and you've learned how to combine them into pleasing combinations. You can choose a monochromatic color scheme, or one that is complementary or analogous. Do you remember what these words mean? If not, take a few minutes to reread "Introduction to Color" in activity 5A.

There's one more color that is often used in flower arrangements—white. White combines with every color! Use a white vase as a base for any arrangement. Use small white flowers as filler behind larger flowers. White can brighten up any color and make the arrangement more exciting.

White can be used all alone as well. A garden of all white flowers is called a moon garden, because it shines brightly in the moonlight even in the middle of the night. Arrangements of all white flowers are often used traditionally for weddings.

We sometimes describe colors by tints, tones, and shades. A **tint** of a color is made by adding white to the color. For example, adding white to red makes pink. A **tone** is made by adding gray to a color; dusty rose is a tone made by adding gray to red. A **shade** of color is made by adding black to the color; burgundy is a shade of red. Primary colors can be blended with secondary colors to create tertiary or intermediate colors. You can see the blending of colors in the tertiary color wheel.

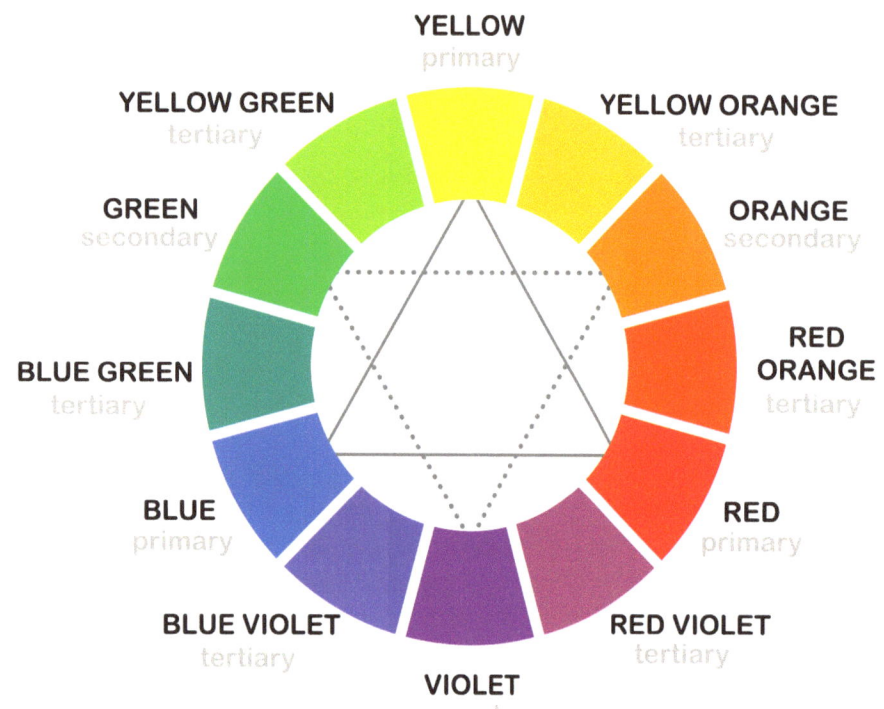

Primary Color Wheel

Try This

Cut out pictures of different flowers from a magazine or seed catalog. Separate them into six piles, one for each color. Then combine them in different ways to illustrate monochromatic, complementary, and analogous color combinations.

Which color combinations do your friends and family like best? Make a display of monochromatic, complementary, and analogous color combinations using the flower pictures you cut out. Ask your friends and family to vote on their favorite color combination. Did everyone like the same one best? Did most people like analogous combinations rather than complementary combinations? Which one do you like the best?

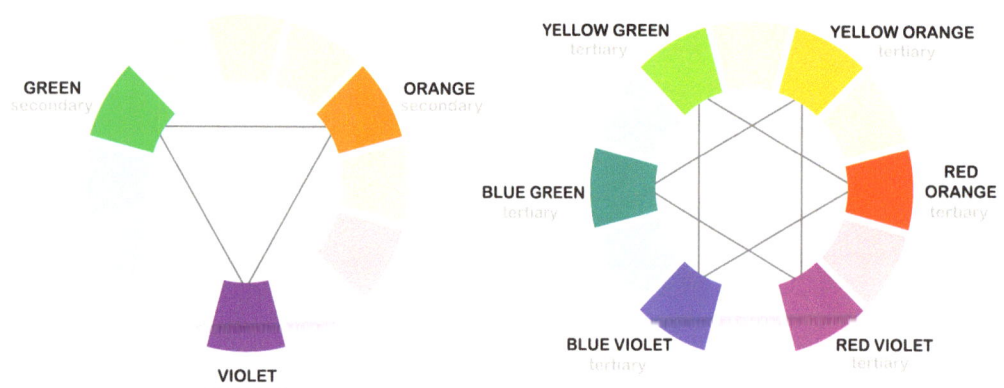

Secondary Color Wheel   **Tertiary Color Wheel**

30 / Floriculture Leader and Youth Education, Grades 3–4

Blooms A-Round

ACTIVITY 5B

Materials Needed:
- Plant materials: flowers and greenery
- Scissors
- Vase or container to hold arrangement (clean)

Time Needed:
- 1 hour

An Arrangement

An arrangement is any group of flowers placed in a container according to a plan. This plan is called the **design.** The flowers and plants of the arrangement and the container should look like they belong together. They should have similar themes, for example, spring flowers in a spring basket or dried flowers on a piece of driftwood. When this happens, the arrangement has harmony and will be pleasing to look at.

Form is the basic outline or shape of your arrangement. Some basic forms for flower arrangements are rectangles or squares, circles or ovals, and triangles. You should consider the container and the use of the arrangement when deciding what form your design will be.

When planning your design, you should also consider balance in the arrangement. **Balance** is the placement of flowers and foliage so that the arrangement looks stable and not like it might fall over. **Symmetry** is also important. An arrangement is symmetrical when both sides of the arrangement are very similar or equal. A holiday centerpiece would be an example of a symmetrical and balanced arrangement.

- *Life Skill:*
  Practicing creativity, completing a task, valuing diversity, making decisions, visualizing information

- *Project Skill*
  Flower presentation

Now What? / 31

Try This

Part 1: Round Arrangement

You will create a simple round arrangement. The form of the design should be circular, balanced, and symmetrical. The finished arrangement should have a full look. Use one kind of flower with greenery, or use several kinds of flowers with only one type of foliage. Remember that color is important, and the flowers and greenery selected should harmonize with each other and the container.

First, working with your helper, plan your floral design and gather your supplies. The container used for the arrangement should be wide, shallow, and clean and full of water with floral preservative. You will need several stems of flowers.

Determine which flowers will be in the center of your circular design. The stems of those flowers should be about 1 and 1 1/2 times the width and the height of the container. Place these in the container, then add additional flower stems to the arrangement. Arrange the flowers so they face all directions. Make sure the filler flowers and greenery hide all the individual stems. You can extend some of the plant materials over the edge of the container to help add depth and hide the edges. Check your arrangement for balance and symmetry.

Choosing Flowers

When selecting flowers to purchase from a florist, grocery story, or wholesale supplier, there are some things to look for. These are some of the same things you learned when harvesting flowers to use for arrangements from your own garden. Flowers should look healthy, with no disease or damage to the flowers or leaves. There should not be any drooping flowers or leaves, and the colors of the flowers should be bright. Look for flowers that haven't opened fully, because this allows them to live longer in your arrangement. Avoid flowers that look as though they are old, unhealthy, or losing leaves or petals.

Fig. 1. Place greenery to frame in the arrangement and define the round shape.

Fig. 2. Place the focal flowers.

Fig. 3. Fill in around the focal flowers with the filler flowers.

Part 2: Bud Vase

Look at the instructions for a simple bud vase in activity 5A. This time, with your helper, think about combining colors and shape by using either two colors of the same kind of focal flower, or two kinds of focal flower in the same color. For example, use a pink rose and two pink carnations or one red rose and two white roses. The form of this design is vertical.

Blossoming Discoveries

Tell your project helper how you made your arrangement.

_____
_____
_____

Explain why it is important to think about matching colors and shapes in an arrangement.

_____
_____
_____

Describe what you learned about using colors and shapes when being creative.

_____
_____
_____

In the future how can you use what you learned about combining colors to choose colors in other projects?

_____
_____
_____

Dig Deeper

Go to several florists and investigate the following. Report your findings in a notebook or poster, or share with your friends or parents.

- **Quality of flowers available for purchase**
  Talk with the florist and see if they have some old or dying flowers that you could compare to fresh healthy ones.
- **Selection of different types of flowers**
  Look at all the kinds of flowers available to use for arrangements.
- **Different kinds of flowers on display**
  Investigate how different kinds of flowers are used in different types of arrangements, and how they are used together in the same arrangements.
- **Colors of flowers used in arrangements**
  Are they complementary, analogous? (Go to "Color" in Activity 5A for information.) See if you can find an arrangement that is not symmetrical. Was it pleasing to look at? Look for examples of balanced and unbalanced arrangements.

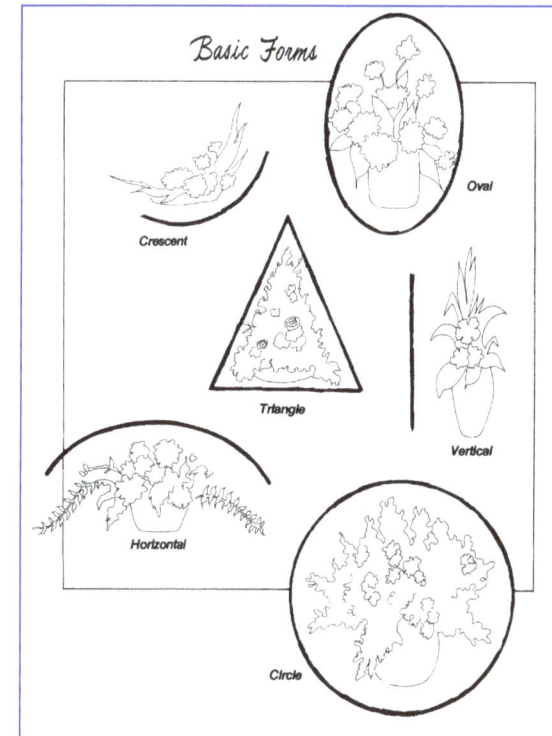

Basic Forms: Crescent, Oval, Triangle, Vertical, Horizontal, Circle

Now What? / 33

Imagine That

An Introduction to Floriculture

ACTIVITY 6A

Look at and learn about the **floriculture** world around you. Start by thinking about what you have learned so far about the field of floriculture. By now, you may know how to plan, plant, and grow flowers. You may also have made a simple flower arrangement. Now it is time to learn what careers are associated with these activities. One of the best ways to do this is to talk with a person who has a career in floriculture.

- Life Skill:
  Navigating in your environment, communicating, building relationships
- Project Skill:
  Learning about careers

Materials Needed:
- Paper
- Pencil

Time Needed:
- 1 hour

Try This

You can learn about careers in floriculture through the following suggested activities. You only need to pick one to complete the project, but do more if you are interested.
- Visit a florist or floral wholesaler: Arrange to have the florist do a demonstration and find out about his or her career and where he/she gets their flowers.
- Visit a nursery or commercial greenhouse : Talk about the nursery and retail aspect of floriculture, and how they grow and care for plants.
- Visit a public garden or conservatory: Talk with the director or plant curator about the function of the garden or conservatory. Look especially to see plant combinations and color schemes used at the conservatory or garden.

When visiting a business, a florist, or a garden, ask people working there to tell you about their jobs. You should also ask the following questions:
- What do you do every day?
- How did you decide to become a (florist, gardener, greenhouse operator, etc.)?
- What do you like best about your job? Is there any part that you don't like?
- What sorts of things should I learn or study if I am interested in this career?

With your helper, discuss other questions you might ask. Read the section on Interviewing Tips on the next page before you go to your interview.

34 / Floriculture Leader and Youth Education, Grades 3–4

Blossoming Discoveries

Tell your project helper what you learned about careers in floriculture.

_____
_____
_____
_____

Describe why it is important to learn about careers in floriculture.

_____
_____
_____
_____

What did you find out that you will need to learn to have a career in floriculture?

_____
_____
_____
_____

In the future, how can you use what you learned about careers in floriculture?

_____
_____
_____

Dig Deeper

1. Make a list of some things you think you will need to learn to have a career in floriculture. How will you learn these things?

2. Why is it important to study many different subjects in school? For a career in floriculture will you need to know about more than plants?

Interviewing tips:

Be prepared. Write down the questions you want to ask ahead of time. Ask the person you want to interview if it is OK to ask him or her some questions. You may even want to call ahead and schedule a time to meet. Be polite to the person you are interviewing. Ask a question and wait patiently for an answer. Don't interrupt when the other person is talking. It is best to interview lots of people instead of just one. See how the responses from each person are similar and different from the other answers you got.

Imagine That / 35

Plants Around the World

ACTIVITY 6B

Throughout history, people have used flowers to communicate with each other. A common example is a red rose for love. Flowers are used in many different ways in cultures around the world. For example, a yellow rose sometimes means friendship and happiness, but in some cultures it may be seen as a sign to start a fight or to show jealousy.

Plants and flowers can also be grown differently in other parts of the world. For example, the poinsettia is often grown as an annual plant for holiday decorating, but in tropical areas it grows year round and is sometimes a shrub in a yard or garden.

 **Life Skill:**
Valuing diversity, practicing creativity

 **Project Skill:**
Discover the uses of plants in other cultures

Materials Needed:
- Paper
- Pencil
- Internet to search for information

Time Needed:
- 30 minutes

Try This

Investigate a flower or plant of interest to you, but not commonly seen or used in your community. Include a photo or drawing of the flower or plant and tell how it might be used and why.

Flower or plant I investigated	
Resources I used to find information	
Origin of the plant, where it is found	
Some uses of the plant and why it's used in that way	
Drawing or picture of plant	

36 / Floriculture Leader and Youth Education, Grades 3–4

Blossoming Discoveries

Describe to your project helper what you learned about how plants are used in other cultures.

_____
_____
_____
_____

List three reasons why it is important to learn and appreciate the uses of plants in other cultures.

_____
_____
_____
_____

What three things did you learn about valuing diversity and knowing new things about other cultures?

_____
_____
_____
_____

Describe how, in the future, you can use what you learned about other cultures' differences to improve your community.

_____
_____
_____

Dig Deeper

1. Choose a culture different from your own to find out more information on the many uses of plants. Using the Internet, write a report about that culture, making sure to include information about the uses of plants for food, fiber, and medicine.

2. Using the Internet, find a recipe from another culture that you want to try that has a new herb or different way to use a plant. Get your parents or helper to help you make the recipe. Share what you made with family and friends.

People have been interested in flowers for thousands of years because they are so pretty and often smell wonderful. Many customs and traditions that go along with flowers go back to before recorded history. One of the oldest customs (more than 50,000 years old) is placing flowers on the grave of a loved one as a sign of remembering and respect.

In Victorian times, people used symbols and gestures, in addition to words, to communicate. Flowers took on specific meanings. Today, these meanings are largely forgotten. When we give a gift of flowers, it is meant to show thoughtfulness and love. Most flowers also have traditional meanings. Here are some of the flowers the Victorians used, and examples of their meanings. What do you think a gift of pansies and zinnias would mean? Make up some combinations that would express your feelings when you give flowers to your mother, brother, sister, teacher, or leader.

apple blossom	promise	orchid	delicate beauty
baby's breath	festivity	pansy	loving thoughts
bachelor's button	anticipation	rose	
black-eyed susan	encouragement	pink	friendship
carnation		red	passionate love
pink	gratitude	red & white	unity
red	flashy	white	purity
white	remembrance	snapdragon	presumptuous
yellow	cheerful	statice	success
daisy	innocence	sunflower	adoration
geranium	comfort	sweetpea	shyness
gladiolus	strength of character	tulip	
iris	inspiration	pink	caring
lavender	distrust	purple	royalty
lilac	first love	red	declaration of love
lily		white	forgiveness
calla	regal	yellow	hopelessly in love
day	enthusiasm	violet	faithfulness
stargazer	ambition	zinnia	thoughts of friends

Imagine That / 37

Glossary

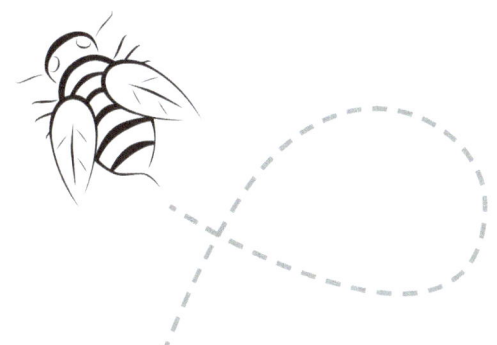

A

Annual: A plant that completes its entire life cycle in a single year or growing season

Anther: The top-most part of the stamen, where pollen is produced

Arrangement: The result of combining flowers and greenery in a confined space (e.g., a vase)

B

Balance: An aspect of a flower arrangement where there are equal amounts of plant material on both or all sides of the center of an arrangement

Bud Vase: A simple vertical design in a tall, slender vase. (The size of the container's neck will limit the number of stems you can use. These are usually one-sided designs.)

C

Color wheel: A circular representation of colors used to divide them into categories based upon their origin (e.g., the color orange is placed between the colors red and yellow on the color wheel, because it originated from the combination of those two colors)

Complementary colors: Colors located directly opposite one another on the color wheel (e.g., purple and yellow, orange and blue, and red and green)

Compost: A mixture of decayed (rotten) plant matter that is like food for soil; also helps keep soil light and fluffy

Conclusion: A step in the scientific method in which you evaluate your results

Conditioning: The process of preparing cut plant materials so that they live longer in an arrangement

Cotyledon: A structure that contains temporary food for the embryo until leaves form and the plant can make its own food

Cutting garden: A flower garden with flowers that do well when they are cut to be used in floral arrangements

E

Embryo: The undeveloped plant in the seed; a tiny plant complete with leaf, stem, and root parts

Exoskeleton: The hard, outer, protective shell of an insect

Experiment: A test under controlled conditions that is made to see if a hypothesis (guess) is right or wrong

F

Filler flower: Smaller flowers (e.g., baby's breath, statice, or heather) in an arrangement that are less dramatic in color than the focal flower; used to fill in areas where flowers and/or greenery are lacking to make an arrangement seem more full

Floriculture: The art of growing and caring for flowers and ornamental crops

Flower: Often the showy, colorful, reproductive structure of a plant; produces seeds

Flower preservative: A substance used to keep cut flowers and foliage alive longer than normal

Focal flower: The flower in an arrangement that provides color and a center of interest

Form: The basic outline or shape of an arrangement; forms may be horizontal, vertical, circular, triangular, or even oval

Fruit: The part of a plant that holds the seeds

G

Germination: The process by which a seed takes in water and swells and in which the embryo begins to grow

Greenery: Plant material lacking flowers (e.g., leather leaf, asparagus fern, etc.) used as a background in floral arrangements

H

Harmony: An aspect of a flower arrangement where the combinations of color and plant materials, among other things, make the arrangement pleasing to look at

Hue: The general name for all primary colors (red, yellow, blue), secondary colors (orange, green, violet) and tertiary colors (those created by combining a primary color and secondary color)

Hypothesis: A guess of what you think will happen in a given situation, or under a certain set of circumstances

L

Leaf: The part of the plant that makes food

M

Mulch: A ground cover (such as leaves, sawdust, or shredded bark) used to keep moisture in the ground and to prevent weeds from growing near plants

O

Organic matter: The remains of any once-living organism (plants, animals, etc.) used to enrich garden soils; the primary component of compost

Ovary: The female part of a flower that contains the ovules that form seeds when fertilized by pollen; the enlarged base of the pistil

P

Pest: Any animal, insect, or disease that causes harm to your garden

Petal: Often the colorful, showy part of the flower used to attract pollinators

Pinching: The practice of removing the growing tip or tips of a plant to increase the number of shoots coming from a portion of the stem

Pistil: The female part of a flower

Planting depth: The depth in growing medium to place seeds for successful germination; varies for each kind of seed

Pollen: The dust-like grains produced by the anthers on the stamens (male part) of flowers that sticks to the stigmas (female part) of flowers to fertilize the ovule; distributed primarily by wind or insects

Pollinator: Any animal, insect (such as bees and butterflies), or naturally occurring conditions (such as wind) that transfers pollen from the anther of a flower to the stigma

Primary colors: Those colors that cannot be made using a combination of any other colors (e.g., red, blue, and yellow)

R

Root: The part of a plant that grows below the ground as an anchor for the plant and to supply the plant with water and food

S

Scientific method: A series of steps (asking a question, gathering data, making a guess, running an experiment, and reaching a conclusion) used to solve a problem or answer a question

Secondary colors: Those colors that result from the combination of any two primary colors (e.g., orange, green, and purple)

Seed: An embryo packaged along with a store of food within a resistant coat

Seed Coat: The tough, outermost part of a seed

Sepal: A whorl of modified leaves that encloses and protects the flower bud before it opens

Shade: The result of adding black to any hue (e.g., adding black to the hue blue makes navy blue)

Shoot: The above-ground portion of a plant body, consisting of stems, leaves, and flowers

Stamen: The pollen-producing male reproductive organ of a flower, consisting of an anther and filament

Stem: The part of a plant used to transport water, minerals, and food from one part of a plant to another; the part of a plant that makes leaves and holds them up

Stigma: The sticky part at the top of the pistil where pollen lands

Stomata: Tiny pores, often on the undersides of plant leaves, that let gasses in and out

Symmetry: An aspect of a flower arrangement where both sides look very similar or equal

<u>T</u>

Tint: The result of adding white to any hue (e.g., adding white to the hue red makes pink)

Tone: The result of adding gray to any hue (e.g., adding gray to the hue red makes "dusty rose")

Transplant: Young plants started from seed and grown indoors; these are later planted in the garden

<u>V</u>

Variegation: The natural combination of two or more colors on the foliage of a plant

<u>W</u>

Weed: Any plant growing where it is not wanted (e.g., a dandelion growing in your cutting garden)

References

4-H Entomology 1: Creepy Crawlies, 4H CCS BU-6853, Purdue University Cooperative Extension System, West Lafayette, Indiana.

4-H Garden Floriculture A: See Them Sprout, 4H CCS BU-7162, Purdue University Cooperative Extension System, West Lafayette, Indiana.

Add Hours to Your Flowers, HO-158-W, Purdue University Cooperative Extension System, West Lafayette, Indiana.

Record Sheet

Name _____ Birthdate _____

Address _____ City _____ Zip _____

Township _____ 4-H Club _____

County _____ Years in project _____ Years in 4-H _____

4-H-er should review *Floriculture: Leader and Youth Education, Grades 3-4* and record activities that were completed this year. 4-H Leader should check activity and initial on the line. Youth should complete at least 5 Try This or Dig Deeper activities per year. If possible, youth should complete all 6 activities each year.

"A" activities for 3rd grade	Date Completed Month/Day/Year	Helper Initials	"B" activities for 4th grade	Date Completed Month/Day/Year	Helper Initials
1. Let's Plan 1A. Somewhere Over the Rainbow...Garden	___/___/___	___	**1. Let's Plan** 1B. A Cut Above the Rest	___/___/___	___
2. Dig In 2A. Digging in...the Soil	___/___/___	___	**2. Dig In** 2B. Transplants for a Speedy Start	___/___/___	___
3. While You Wait 3A. Blooming Seeds	___/___/___	___	**3. While You Wait** 3B. Flower Power	___/___/___	___
4. Watch Out 4A. Healthy Plant Parts	___/___/___	___	**4. Watch Out** 4B. What's Buggin' You?	___/___/___	___
5. Now What? 5A. A Blooming Rainbow	___/___/___	___	**5. Now What?** 5B. Blooms A-Round	___/___/___	___
6. Imagine That 6A. An Introduction to Floriculture	___/___/___	___	**6. Imagine That** 6B. Plants Around the World	___/___/___	___

Title of Action Demo _____

Location of Action Demo _____

4-H Member's Signature _____

4-H Leader's Signature _____

About the Author

Kathryn S. Orvis is a professor and associate head of the Horticulture and Landscape Architecture Department at Purdue University. A nationally recognized leader in horticultural education, she integrates teaching, Extension, and research to engage youth through gardening, plant science, and urban agriculture. She has authored more than twenty peer-reviewed articles, book chapters, and curricula, securing more than $1 million in grants. Her honors include an American Society for Horticultural Science (ASHS) Outstanding Undergraduate Educator Award and a Purdue Cooperative Extension Specialist Career Award. Orvis's work focuses on using plants to teach plant science, STEM, and a variety of life skills.

www.ingramcontent.com/pod-product-compliance
Lightning Source LLC
Chambersburg PA
CBHW061031180426
43194CB00037B/111